Resurrecting the Living:
My Personal Journey Through Grief, Loss and Depression

Roblynne McDuffie

Copyright ©2018 by Roblynne McDuffie

All rights reserved. No part of this publication may be reproduced, stored in retrieval system, or transmitted by any form or by any means – electronic, mechanic, digital, photocopy, recording, or any other – without the prior permission of the publisher.

Burkwood Media Group

P O Box 29448

Charlotte, NC 28229

www.burkwoodmedia.com

Printed in the United States

ISBN: 978-0-692-15733-6

Table of Contents

Acknowledgements..i

Dedication...ii

1. How It All Began 1
2. The Domino Effect 24
3. Existing in the "Dark Place" 37
4. Coping With Emotions in Your Own Time 50
5. Surrounding Yourself With Positive People 68
6. Overcoming Your Pain By Encouraging Others 76
7. Resurrecting the Living.....................................86

About The Author.. 99

Acknowledgements

I would like to Acknowledge the following people:

Mrs. Erika Holifield of Erika Holifield Photography on such an awesome photoshoot for my book cover and website!

The Charlotte Write to Publish group for their continuous support, encouragement, inspiration, and expertise throughout my journey in becoming a new author.

My publisher, Burkwood Media for believing my story could reach more people dealing with grief, to publish it.

All my friends and loved ones who helped me through this journey as well. There are far too many to name, but you know who you are.

Dedication

This book is dedicated to my late mother, Mrs. Jacqueline Johnson Quarles, also known to her friends as "Jackie-Joe" and a self-proclaimed "Bad Mamma-Jamma;" to my late father, Mr. Robert Wiley McDuffie; to my Aunt Homazella and Uncle Buster, who both assisted in raising me to be the woman I am today; and to the memory of all of those who were a part of my "village" of parental figures and caregivers.

Chapter 1

How It All Began

Many would say that my personal experiences with grief and loss should warrant an extended stay in an insane asylum—or even ending my own life. There have been moments when I felt at least a small urge to lean toward both options. I've never felt so lost in my entire life. It's as though my world has been flipped upside down, and I am continuing to fall deeper and deeper into an abyss of pain. Anxiety and depression are understatements for what I am experiencing. This feeling sometimes takes a huge toll on my mind, body, and soul, and I don't wish it on my worst enemy.

It was the beginning of the summer of 2013. It was the end of my eighth year as an educator and the end of my second year as a School Counselor. I had not signed my contract for the upcoming school year for various reasons—but the primary one was because my mother had suddenly become very ill. During this time, I had just moved to a city in my home state of South Carolina a year prior, and really didn't care for the new city. However, being that I was new to the School Counseling profession, I was willing to relocate wherever I could gain some experience in my field.

This "new" city—Florence—was about three hours away from my hometown of Greenwood, South Carolina, and a little over an hour from Columbia, South Carolina—which is where I relocated to from Greenwood in 2009. My mother always encouraged me to follow my dreams, and to spread my wings and fly. It was a bittersweet moment when I left Greenwood. While I was somewhat sad to leave my mother and the rest of my family, I knew I had to leave in order to thrive in my career and in life.

I wasn't too worried about my mother's well-being when I left. She and my stepfather were both in pretty good health. Despite one of my aunts' lamentations over me moving out of my hometown and "leaving the family," moving away gave me a level of peace I never had before.

Whenever I talked to Mama on the phone, she seemed so despondent and aloof. The mother I knew had suddenly transformed, almost immediately at the beginning of 2013, into someone I no longer knew nor recognized—although I still loved her with everything in me. Usually, my mother would call every day, three to five times per day. We would discuss my day, I would vent to her about work, and other aspects of my personal life. We would laugh and talk most days. If she was sitting outside on the porch while we were on the phone, she would brag to a passerby "this my daughter on the phone! My baby is smart! She's a guidance counselor and has a Master's degree!" Sometimes, she would even give the phone to the passerby for them to speak to me—which I absolutely hated, and I would fuss at her about it when she came back to the phone.

During this particular summer, my mother and stepfather both began to experience some major health issues. My stepfather was battling kidney failure, and I wasn't sure at the time what my mother was experiencing. All I knew was she'd stopped eating and was losing weight rapidly. I knew in my heart when I visited home that April something was wrong, and she needed my attention. Aside from the sudden weight loss, I noticed my mother displayed a general aura of malaise about her that I'd never witnessed before. She still laughed and talked, but had this deep, sad look in her eyes as though something was wrong. Every time I talked to her on the phone, she always sounded tired—but chalked it up to "allergies" or "a bad cold."

I knew she was visiting her doctor regularly for her diabetes and high blood pressure. She always assured me she was taking care of herself. However, during this visit to Greenwood, I made up in my mind as soon as school was out that following month, I was going to get her some medical assistance elsewhere. In the meantime, my relatives who lived near her would keep an eye on her until I could finish out the school year. She was still mobile, and able to care for her basic needs to a certain extent.

Also, shortly before this same visit home, my stepbrother had moved my stepfather in with him so that he and his wife could care for him. Our plan was to move my mother and stepfather into a senior apartment community together, but God had other plans.

As soon as school was out, I went to Greenwood and took my mother to Aiken, South Carolina. I wanted to try a different healthcare system to see what was really going on with her. She was very resistant and didn't want me to help her—but at this point, it was apparent she was no longer able to care for herself. I became the "mother" and she became the "child."

The summer started out promising. Once I got my mother to Aiken, she started looking better in just a matter of weeks—although she still seemed to struggle with her appetite and the doctors couldn't figure out why. After almost a month in the hospital, and some small progress with regaining her appetite, I approved she be moved to a nursing home until I figured out whether I would remain in Florence or relocate back to Columbia. Also, I wanted to make sure she was in an environment where she would receive 24-hour treatment and medical attention.

As the weeks went by, however, my mother's health seemed to decline very rapidly again—this time, at an all-time low. She stopped eating. Prior to this "sudden, mysterious" illness, she stood at 5'5" and weighed about 150 pounds. Her weight dropped to 95 pounds in a matter of months, and she became so weak that she eventually stopped walking and was no longer able to stand. I would travel to Aiken a few days a week and visit her. It would make her day; however, I would become more and more distraught after each visit because of her noticeable decline.

Then one day, I received a call from the nursing home, informing me I had to get to Aiken immediately. My mother had been rushed to the hospital. Her breathing was very labored and she wasn't expected to make it past the next 24 hours. She had developed pneumonia and sepsis. A friend drove me down, and a few family members also came that night. Fortunately, her condition improved slightly the next day, enough for her to be able to laugh and talk and even crack a few jokes.

I was relieved and thanked God for improving her health within those 24 hours. Unfortunately, the next month turned out to be pure mental, and emotional anguish for me. During this same time, I decided not to sign my contract for the following school year, so I could care for her. I also wanted to find a job in Columbia, where I would be closer. Columbia was always familiar to me, and I had a lot of close friends and loved ones there. It was a giant leap of faith because I didn't have another job lined up prior to resigning; but, I knew in my heart I made the right decision. I would go through the cycle of spending a week at the hospital with her, and then coming home for a couple of days to get some real rest and continue to look for jobs. She couldn't rest at night and would be up screaming in pain.

Then one day—there came an explanation to all of her suffering. The doctor did a CT scan in order to see whether the pneumonia had cleared up completely. During the CT scan, he discovered a large cancerous mass that consumed the majority of my mother's liver, as well as more cancerous growths throughout her chest cavity. He insisted on running another test in order to see where the cancer originated from, as well as her prognosis.

During this same week, my stepfather—who had also been in and out of the hospital all that summer—wasn't expected to live much longer. My stepsister informed me his kidney failure had run its course and there was nothing else the doctors could do for him. They would possibly be placing him in Hospice by the end of that week.

With everything going on, I was emotionally numb. In addition to all of this, I had a job interview in Columbia this same week. There were a series of events that occurred on the day of the interview. I interviewed for the job and it was my best interview ever; I have no idea how, because all of my nerves were completely shot. I went to Aiken immediately after my interview, and the doctor informed me my mother had stage 4 metastatic cancer that originated from either her pancreas or colon and there was nothing else he could do other than suggest Hospice. Additionally, my stepsister updated me on the fact that my stepfather would be placed in Hospice the next day. We arranged for them both to go in on the next day and for their rooms to be next door to each other. On August 23rd—my stepfather was placed in HospiceCare of Greenwood in the morning, and my mother was placed there in the afternoon.

That night, my stepsister called me from my stepfather's room and suggested I put the phone to my mother's ear. She put her phone to her father's ear and my mother—in her shallow, very weak voice—said "Hey Wilbur. I love you." According to my stepsister, his face lit up, although he couldn't speak. The next day, August 24th, he passed away. When I told my mother, she just said "ok" and went back to sleep. Later in the evening, she woke up and said, "Wilbur gone, ain't he?" I said "yeah, Mama, he's gone." She then softly proclaimed, "Oh Lord" and went back to sleep. I spent the next three days watching my mother literally sleep her life away.

Resurrecting The Living

She would wake up about three times a day and yell in pain. The Hospice nurses would come and give her more morphine, which would help her sleep. During one of those days, my mother's friend since childhood, Miss Ann, urged me to go and take a break for a few hours as she sat with my mother. Also, many friends and loved ones came to visit my mother and me. Those visits were truly comforting, and some would even bring lunch or dinner.

The day before she passed away, I was sitting on the side of her bed holding her hand. Around that same time, one of the pastors of my family's church came to visit. The pastor was talking to me about "releasing" my mother to God so she wouldn't continue to try and hold on for me. At first, I was thinking to myself, "so—I'm telling my mama it's okay for her to die. But it's not okay with me!" But as I was processing the pastor's words in my mind, it dawned on me that my mother was suffering and trying to "hold on" for me. It was selfish of me to continue to subject her to so much suffering and pain.

By the time the pastor explained this to me thoroughly, my mother woke up—of course, in excruciating pain. I continued to hold her hand, and I began the most difficult conversation I ever had in my life. I told her "Mama—I appreciate every single thing you have done for me in my life; how you have raised me to be the woman I am. I don't want you to suffer anymore, so go ahead and rest in The Arms of Jesus now. I will be just fine. I will miss you, but I will see you again someday." Her reply was "but I don't wanna let you go." As I fought back tears, because I didn't want her to see me cry, I told her "but you're suffering waaay too much and I don't want you to suffer anymore. I'm going to be fine—I promise." I continued to tell her how much I loved her, and how I will see her again someday. She never said anything else. I stroked her hand as the nurse came in and gave her more morphine. After about 30 minutes, she fell asleep. She only opened her eyes once more, later that afternoon when one of my aunts told her "Lynne's gonna be ok. We're gonna take very good care of her. I love you." She could no longer talk, but she fell back asleep and never awakened after that.

Later that night, the Hospice nurses asked if I wanted them to turn her on her side so that I could sleep next to her one last time. I agreed, and they turned her on her left side. I fell asleep beside my mother for the very last time and had my arm around her the whole night. A part of me didn't

Resurrecting The Living

want to let her go, while another part of me wanted to comfort her as she was beginning her inevitable transition from this world.

The very next night—August 27th—around 10:40pm, I was on the side of the bed with one hand on her forehead, and my other hand holding her hands to her chest; her hands were crossed over each other. I was getting ready to pray for the night. As soon as "Father God—in The Name of Jesus" slipped from my tongue, she took her last five breaths. I called the nurse after the first one because they were so paused. The nurse stayed with me, and after the fifth breath, my mother didn't take anymore. About a minute later, the nurse checked her pulse and confirmed she had passed away. Of course, I wailed very loudly as one of the nurses rubbed my back. My best friend in the whole wide world, the one who knew me better than I knew myself, the one who I confided in about everything in my life, the one who was my biggest cheerleader in all of my life's endeavors—had transitioned away from this world. Just as she had brought me into this world and witnessed me take my very first breath, I was by her side as she took her last.

That night, several relatives from both my fathers' and stepfathers' sides of my family came to Hospice to be with me. When the funeral home attendant came to pick up her body, he asked me if I wanted to say anything else to my mother before he took her body. I stated, very matter-of-factly "I've said everything I needed to say to her while she was still alive."

Chapter 2

The Domino Effect

A few months had passed by and I was just beginning to ease into a "new normal" after losing my mother and stepfather within three days of each other. And then I received a call from one of my cousins while I was at work, informing me that my Aunt Homazella—who was my mother's oldest sister—had a stroke, and it paralyzed one side of her body. After hearing this news, I broke down in tears, as one of my coworkers comforted me.

Resurrecting The Living

Aunt Homazella took me into her home when I was 13 years old, around the time my mother was beginning to battle drug addiction. My mother would have other people in the house who were also using drugs. I didn't feel safe around those people, although I didn't know or understand exactly what was going on at the time. I didn't understand why my mother and those people would go and hide in the back bedroom of our apartment and eventually emerge from the room "disoriented and very aloof." My instincts were telling me to remove myself from that environment. I also discovered a plastic grocery bag of homemade "pipes" hidden under my pillow;

I later learned they were pipes used to smoke crack cocaine. My mother denied any knowledge of how they ended up there. My aunt agreed to allow me to live with her during my teenage years. She assisted in raising me from the time I was born. She had a heart of gold and would do anything in the world for anyone.

As much as I loved my mother, our relationship wasn't very stable during my teenage years. At the time, I was ashamed of her drug addiction and wanted her to change for the better. However, I didn't know how to help her and didn't realize that shunning her was more detrimental than beneficial.

Resurrecting The Living

As I became an adult and moved away for college, our relationship improved tremendously. I started surrounding myself with people of various perspectives on life, and I apologized to my mother for the way I treated her. From that moment on, she became my best friend again, as she was during my childhood prior to my teenage years. Aunt Homazella provided food, shelter, love and spiritual growth when I was a teenager—though she sometimes enforced very strict rules.

That chilly November day in 2013, I rushed to Greenwood after work; I was working in Columbia at the job I interviewed for the day before my mother and stepfather were moved to Hospice. I had just relocated back to Columbia from Florence the same week. My aunt couldn't speak clearly, but she could say my name, and she knew who I was. She was happy to see me! I kissed her and sat and talked with my cousins before heading back to Columbia. Each day, my cousins would keep me posted and tell me she's doing okay. About a week later, I received a call from a relative, informing me her condition had taken a sudden turn for the worse, and she was being moved to Hospice. Of course, I had an emotional breakdown, knowing she was coming

Resurrecting The Living

to her end. Two days later—which was eight days after her stroke—she passed away.

Our family dynamics changed drastically. Now, our Uncle Buster was the only surviving elderly relative. We all—particularly, his son—pitched in to try and help him survive and thrive without his last two surviving sisters being around anymore. Their youngest sister, my Aunt Shirley, had passed away 13 years prior. We would take Uncle Buster out to lunch or dinner, or out of town in order to get him out of the house and spend some time with him.

On our last road trip, he and I went to Asheville, North Carolina and he was delighted just to be out riding around and looking at the picturesque mountains. He didn't even want to go on any type of spectacular excursions. I wanted to take him to the Biltmore House, since neither he nor I had ever been before. He just wanted to sit in the mall at the food court and people-watch while I did a little shopping. Then, he wanted to go to a buffet. His favorite place was Ryan's and though the foodie in me was looking at him sideways for wanting to eat there (I really wanted to try something local and exclusive to Asheville) I obliged because I wanted to do whatever satisfied him. Such a trip would seem trivial to most, but it meant the world to Uncle Buster. He didn't get around very well in his last 6 years of life due to having surgery on both of his knees, so he would mainly stay at home, go to doctor's visits, or go to the store. We even went to visit some of our close relatives in Spartanburg, South Carolina when we left Asheville and before we headed back to Greenwood that day.

However, Uncle Buster sunk deeper and deeper into a depressed state of mind, dealing with the loss of his sisters, as well as the loss of his significant other at the beginning of 2015. Suddenly one day, in

October of 2015, I received a call from a relative that he passed away from a massive heart attack.

Uncle Buster was like a father to me. He was always there for all of my major life events and was very supportive of all of my dreams and ambitions. After his death, I felt completely lost and alone in this world—as I had suffered the loss of all my surviving parental figures.

My visits to Greenwood have been a major emotional and psychological adjustment for me. At least for two years after my mother, stepfather, and Aunt Homazella passed away, I could visit with

Resurrecting The Living

Uncle Buster and spend time with him. However, once Uncle Buster passed away, everything changed for me—AGAIN. Actually, everything changed for our entire family. Now, we had no surviving elderly relatives anymore. Our elders were the glue that continuously held our family together. I will not sugarcoat the truth—for some time, our family fell apart to an extent. Some of us played the blame game with each other as far as faulting someone for our relatives' deaths. In one instance, one of my cousins and I got into a major disagreement regarding some family property. We eventually reconciled. Even through reconciliation,

I still long for going to visit Aunt Homazella and having Sunday dinner with the family. I miss seeing my mother, Uncle Buster, and my stepfather Wilbur whenever I was in Greenwood. Their proximity to one another made my visits even more special, with my mother and Wilbur living just 5 houses down the street from Aunt Homazella. Also, Uncle Buster had moved in with Aunt Homazella shortly after his knee surgery. After stopping by my mother's house first upon arriving in Greenwood, I would go to Aunt Homazella's house—and then my mother would walk right up to her house, so we would all catch up some more. Uncle Buster and I would

Resurrecting The Living

always get a good laugh out of my mother's daily spats with Aunt Homazella. It was the perfect set-up for all of us.

Prior to losing my last four surviving parental figures—I had experienced losing my grandmother, my father, a few aunts and uncles, and my only brother, in addition to a few other close family friends and loved ones. Although their deaths occurred during various time periods, and they all played a role in raising me, nothing quite compares to losing one family member right after the other in a very short time period. It's as though the Grim Reaper came, and just played this horrible game of dominoes with our family. No matter how bad I wanted my life to be normal again, things just kept falling apart.

Chapter 3

Existing in the "Dark Place"

Over the two years after Uncle Buster's death, and four years after my mother's, aunt's and stepfather's deaths, I gained almost 50 pounds; it didn't help that I was already morbidly obese and at the 300-pound mark prior to their deaths.

I also started becoming angry—a LOT. Life just wasn't fair. I hated my life and what it had suddenly become. Despite the fact I had friends and family to lean on emotionally, all of the people I considered my parental figures were gone. My life was in shambles and I didn't know which way to turn. I would pray, I would cry, I would scream, I would throw and break things in the house. I would curse, I would fall on the floor and curl up into the fetal position and just wail. And most of the time—no one else knew about it but God. I would post certain statuses on social media and then people would inbox me out of concern for my mental and emotional state of mind. Their concerns were legitimate. I just didn't know how to articulate the pain without sounding like I had completely lost my mind, which I probably had, to some degree.

I started to feel like a burden on my friends and loved ones. If I started crying or expressing my emotions in some other way, I would get frustrated when people made me feel as though I was crazy. In my mind, I understood they had not been in my situation, and therefore, it wasn't their fault that they just didn't "get it." I became angry with my mother, stepfather, aunt and uncle for passing away and "leaving me." I thought to myself "how dare they leave me to fend for myself in this crazy thing called life? Some of them even left me without saying goodbye and it wasn't fair!" I got mad at God. I hated my life. I wanted to go into complete hiding from the world. I wanted everybody to leave me alone. I was just done with everything and everybody.

Then, I sunk into a deep depression. I am usually a social butterfly; however, I went back into my "cocoon" during this period. I continued to suffer with feelings of guilt, anger and loneliness. There were times I really didn't want to live life anymore.

The word "exist" is defined as "living, especially under adverse conditions." Some synonyms are

Resurrecting The Living

"surviving," "subsisting," "making do," "getting by," and "managing." This word was the perfect definition of my life shortly after my family members' deaths. I got up every morning, showered, got dressed, went to work, ate when I was hungry, performed my duties at work as consciously as I possibly could, went to bed at night, and repeated the process the next day. On weekends and during holidays off, I slept or just sat at home in silence and solitude. I would talk to friends and family when they called and checked on me, but I didn't really want to leave the house. I didn't want to be bothered. I sank into a dark place.

I resided in that dark place for so long that I became complacent there and didn't want to leave. Sure, I smiled and carried on throughout each day as though I was perfectly fine. But deep inside, I was suffering from this deep depression I rarely talked about because I felt those closest to me couldn't really understand. Even other family members couldn't truly understand. I appreciated the family and friends who were there for me. They tried to understand. Many of them just offered a listening ear, and that's all I needed. I still do from time to time, even now.

Resurrecting The Living

I reached a point where I got tired of people telling me to "pray about it." I always prayed my routine daily prayers to God of thanks and protection. However, I stopped praying for myself while in that dark place. I just existed. I didn't want to live anymore—in a mental, emotional, and spiritual sense. Although I never devised a plan of committing suicide, there were instances when I had vague thoughts of wanting to die; however, I immediately sought therapy during these few instances. This dark place had actually become my best friend and confidante. I continued to wallow in self-pity and reassurance that no one would ever understand me and what I was going through. I made up in my mind that God was punishing me severely for something I did in my past. I played hypothetical scenarios over and over in my head of how I could've kept my mother alive longer, and what else I could've done for my uncle, aunt and stepfather that would've kept them alive.

I felt all types of guilt. I just knew it was my fault they were gone. I could've visited Greenwood and cooked for Uncle Buster more often. I could've come and checked on my mother more and made arrangements sooner to improve her health. Maybe I could've talked to my stepfather more and told him more than a few times how much I loved and appreciated him. I could've called Aunt Homazella more often. Maybe she died from a broken heart because I didn't call her enough. Maybe they all did. It is all my fault these people left this Earth when they did, and I am a terrible person who doesn't deserve a good life.

I thought about how a few people either contacted me or ran into me when I visited Greenwood during that Spring of 2013, and they would express to me their concerns that something was wrong with my mother. I would accept their concerns, but I was initially at a loss for what exactly I needed to do to help my mother. First of all, she was resistant because she was in denial about being sick. So, any mention of taking her to see a doctor or any type of specialist led to a heated argument which only left me upset and feeling powerless. How can I help someone who didn't even want to admit they were seriously ill?

Regardless to this, certain people made me feel as though it *was* my fault my mother passed away. I had already developed my own guilty thoughts and feelings regarding her illness and death. A couple of family members even said to me "if you hadn't moved Jackie (my mother) out of Greenwood, she would still be living." Another person said, "look like you should've known your mama was sick." Of course, with my plethora of emotions all at once, I had the tendency to lash out at those people because they had no idea of the complexity of my mother's illness and my efforts in trying to offer her some assistance in a "timely" manner.

For a period of time, and even during certain moments now, I internalized these negative comments from others. I just knew they were talking about me and painting a picture of me as neglecting my mother—no matter what I was actually doing behind the scenes to get her some help regarding her health. I'm not exactly sure if my analysis of these people was correct, but it's how I felt at the time.

Along with the process of dealing with these emotions, these sudden losses, and the insensitivity of some people—I isolated myself and fell even further into this "dark place." No matter how much I tried to make myself feel better and get out of this dark place, it took a lot of perseverance, faith, and support of positive people for me to overcome it. It also helped me discover my own inner-strength and particularly the strength I learned from my mother when she was alive. During her last month in the hospital, she made a statement to me one day, "I'm not gonna live, but you will live on with your life." This statement resonates with me every time I am trying to accomplish a goal and want to give up. I can hear her saying this and I can also hear her encouraging me, cheering me on, telling me how smart I am, and making me feel like I can accomplish anything I set my mind to.

Chapter 4

Coping With Emotions
In Your Own Time

Being in this dark place started to take a physical toll on me—aside from the obvious emotional and psychological toll. I became tired of being tired, angry, guilty, and lost. In order to move myself out of the dark place, I knew I had to learn how to cope and be realistic about the absence of my loved ones. I often looked for my family members to come back. It seemed as though they had all gone on this long vacation to some foreign country or just to another part of the United States. I wanted to believe they were just temporarily gone to visit a relative or something. The fact that I often had, and still have to this day, vivid dreams of them solidified for me the fact that they aren't actually "gone."

For example, when I make major life decisions, I pray for God to send me a sign. His sign to me is always in a dream, where my mother or one of my other recently departed relatives expresses their approval or disapproval of a decision I am trying to make. I was considering relocating to Fort Mill, South Carolina from Columbia at the beginning of

2017. I wanted to be closer to some family and friends and live in an area where I felt I could succeed as an aspiring author. I prayed about whether or not moving to Fort Mill was the right decision. As the new school year started in August and I was still at my job in Columbia, my mother came to me in a dream. We were discussing my job situation and she stated to me, just as plain as day, "it's time for you to move on." Then I woke up. In my mind, it was confirmation that it was time for me to leave that particular job and find something new. When my mother was alive, she always gave me sound advice. Now that she's gone, she still gives me sound advice in my dreams. Not many people understood my decision to move, and I hadn't found a job in that area right away. But my peace of mind improved significantly as soon as I made the move.

Whenever I feel sad and as though I can't make it without my mother and my other loved ones, I allow myself to process those emotions in any way that hits me at that particular moment. I cry, I scream into a pillow, I throw things without causing any type of destruction, or I do any combination of the three. Some may find something wrong with expressing emotions the way I do; but once I do it rejuvenates me, cleanses me, and centers me. I am able to think logically again. At times, I feel as though being so emotional is some sort of mental illness. I look at people who rarely cry and wonder how they do it. Sometimes, I wish I could be like them and just "stifle" my emotions. However, that's just not who I am and I have come to accept that about myself. I have to get my tears out or express my emotions in some other way in order to maintain, and in some instances regain, some sort of sanity and re-centering.

Various coping mechanisms are effective for various people. For me, as a Christian, prayer and meditation are also my favorite coping mechanisms. I talk to God about EVERYTHING. I also write letters to Him from time to time, especially during periods when I am experiencing challenges. When I pray or write God a letter, I feel at peace because whatever is on my mind and heart, I now surrender to Him. I do feel as though God hears my prayers and He answers them. Even for those who have other religious and or spiritual beliefs, or none at all, putting your words out into the atmosphere when your mind and heart are heavy can offer an unexplainable degree of peace.

Any type of coping takes persistence and open-mindedness. It is a lifelong process. I have always heard and been told the toughest deaths to cope with are either those of a parent—particularly losing a mother—or those of a child. I lost my father when I was 15 years old, just when we were starting to build an even closer relationship. I was really sad when I lost him, and I still think about him quite often. However—his death, for some reason, didn't quite compare to the death of my mother. I loved them both dearly, but there was something very different about losing my mother. She was my best friend. She was the one who carried me for nine months, which made me close to her heart in a literal and figurative sense. I was her only child, so I had all of her attention most of the time.

The old cliché, "Time heals all wounds" is true to some extent. However, the amount of time it takes for a person to go through the grieving process is a very individualized journey—especially after losing multiple loved ones in a short time span, as in my case. Through my own journey, I chose not to dwell so much on how much time it took me to grieve. Instead, I focused on how I was feeling regarding the passing of my loved one at a given moment.

Also, I focused on what was triggering these thoughts and feelings.

For example, about eight months after my mother and stepfather passed—which was also about five months after my Aunt Homazella had passed—I experienced a sudden emotional meltdown at work in my office. This day, I was very overwhelmed with my workload and when someone placed something else on my desk—I just started crying uncontrollably. A coworker immediately came in and closed my door and comforted me. She contacted my therapist and was able to get me an appointment for later that afternoon. My meltdown was so debilitating that my coworker had to drive me home and I had to take the next day off work.

I did see my therapist later that same day and she enlightened me on the dangers of holding in your grief for too long and trying to "be strong." I felt that being "strong" was the best way for me to deal with the grief I was experiencing. A few months prior, I felt as though it was time for me to stop the crying and sadness and move on with my life. After all, I felt no one would really care to continue listening to me mope about my recent losses. No matter how supportive my friends and loved ones were, I still didn't want to continue to "burden" them with my problems.

So, I held back the tears for a period of about three months. When I became sad, I immediately distracted myself by watching TV or going out with friends. I refused to face my thoughts and feelings head-on and I stifled my emotions. There were even a few people who told me that I need to go ahead and "get over" my grief. And I thought to myself "perhaps they're right."

After this meltdown occurred, I promised myself I would take a mental health day from work

Resurrecting The Living

whenever I felt myself starting to become overwhelmed emotionally. To this day, I still take a day off when needed—especially around my mother's birthday, close to Mothers' Day, and around the anniversary of her passing. One thing many people don't understand, and I didn't really understand initially, is that grief is a lifelong process and doesn't have a set timeline. Throughout a person's life, they will find new ways of grieving a certain loved one. What may have worked one year or one month may not work the next year or the next month.

Grief in general is different for each individual. Some people must cry and display their emotions, while others don't cry and instead, express their grief in other ways, such as working more than usual, reading, writing, or traveling. There is no right or wrong way to grieve, despite what some people may believe. There were people who told me to stop crying so much, while others told me to allow the tears to flow. Well, the latter is what usually works for me because I am a very emotional person. Once I express my emotions, then I feel better. As I stated previously—different ways of grieving work for different people. Each individual must find their own way.

Sometimes, unhealthy thoughts may creep into a person's mind throughout the grieving process. It's normal sometimes to experience thoughts of wanting to be with the recently departed loved one; however, experiencing thoughts of wanting to take one's own life need the immediate attention of a professional. Even if a person's thoughts don't flow to that extent, therapy in general can be beneficial in assisting them through the grieving process.

Moments of grief also occur throughout an individual's lifetime. I recently attended a friend's baby shower and became emotional when she read the card attached to a gift from her mother. It instantly triggered my thoughts of how I truly missed my own mother, and I became really sad for a moment although I didn't cry at that time. As she read the card, I was happy for her; but I instantly thought of the fact that one day if I expect a child, my mother won't be here to write a card for me or express her love for me as her daughter.

Almost anything can trigger a moment of grief. As a single woman, I know one day if I get married, that will be an emotional day for me because I always envisioned my parents and parental figures being a part of my ceremony. It will not be the case for me. I handle each moment as it comes—and as in the case of my friend's baby shower, those moments often occur unexpectedly.

It's important to recognize these moments when they occur, and handle them accordingly and in a healthy manner. I still see a therapist from time to time when necessary. Also, be mindful of times when the effects of grief and loss significantly interfere with your daily life and routines. If it becomes increasingly difficult for you to perform usual daily functions, such as working, bathing, sleeping or eating—it is time to seek immediate help. I considered asking my therapist to prescribe medication for depression, but then I was leery of the possible side effects. Therapy and positive support were paramount for my healing process.

Although periods of "disconnection" from society may help, these are the types of moments when help and some degree of reconnection are pivotal. No grieving individual should go through the process alone. Join a grief support group, contact a therapist—whatever it takes for you to at least begin usual daily functions and self-care again. I can't stress this enough: help is very important and can be very beneficial.

Chapter 5

Surrounding Yourself With Positive People

One significant component of grief is having a positive support system. As most people know, the toughest part of the grieving process is after the death and funeral. I will say, for me, this is when the REAL grieving began and when I needed the right people and voices the most.

Resurrecting The Living

Generally, depending on an individual's and family's culture, the time between a person's death and their funeral can more than likely be filled with lots of distractions. Regardless of how and where the person died, the body must be picked up by the coroner and or funeral home. In the case of an unexpected death, and sometimes even if the death is expected, the shock that permeates through the family is usually placed on the backburner in order for the family to continue making funeral arrangements, etc. Visitors immediately begin to come and visit the family shortly after the person's death and in the days leading up to the funeral or homegoing celebration.

After the funeral, when those visitors are no longer pouring in, everything is quiet. The grieving loved ones are left with their own thoughts and feelings. Only positive energy is helpful to those individuals as they continue to process their loss.

There are people, however, who may make insensitive comments to a grieving person. Shortly after my mother passed away, there were a few people who made statements such as "you shouldn't have moved your mama away (for medical treatment)," or "you should've gotten your mama some help sooner." There was even one person who, thinking they were "joking," stated they were going to stop being around me because everyone around me seems to die. Believe it or not, these are people I had known for most of my life. For them to make such hurtful statements truly cut deeply, and even made me feel more guilty. Early in the grieving process, I already felt as though I hadn't done enough for my mother and other recently departed relatives.

Oftentimes, a grieving person just desires a listening ear. Making statements to them such as "well, they're in a better place now," "I know how you feel," or "they wouldn't want you to be sad" could make the person feel even less supported. The best thing to say is either "sorry for your loss, you are in my prayers or thoughts" or "I am here for you." A while back, one of my friends shared with me that she didn't feel as though she had been much help to me because she never knows what to say. I assured her she has been a tremendous help to me because instead of brushing me off when I'm upset, she is always there to listen intently. A listening ear is much more golden to me than a person who can't quite find the right words to say at a given moment.

Resurrecting The Living

Just as there were negative-spirited people who made such comments to me, there have also been positive-spirited people who constantly remind me of all the help I gave my loved ones and the sacrifices I made. They also remind me of how these family members purposely hid their illnesses from me until the physical effects could no longer be concealed—just because they didn't want me to "worry" about them. Those people are still an integral part of my life today. Some are long-term friends and family members, while others are friends I have made in recent years.

One very interesting concept I have learned, especially since losing my mother, is family isn't always blood relatives. During significant dates, such as my mother's birthday, certain friends and relatives always check on me and may even treat me to lunch or dinner on that day. Family can be anyone a person feels a close, intimate connection with. My circle, or "family," have remained my constant confidantes in recent years. Whenever I need someone just to listen to me cry, they are there for me.

Since my losses, I no longer have the emotional, psychological or spiritual capacity to allow any type

Resurrecting The Living

of negativity into my life and my own personal readjustment. The few negative-spirited people who have come along have either changed for the better or I have had to end that friendship/acquaintance. I focus on the positive voices around me. Even when I don't want to believe that I will make it through each day without my mother and other recently departed loved ones, they continue reiterating the fact that I will and I still have purpose on this Earth in my own life.

Chapter 6

Overcoming Your Pain By Encouraging Others

Personally, I find that helping others who are grieving helps me through my own grieving process. When people experience any type of loss, they usually find comfort in knowing someone else has experienced very similar circumstances. This helps the grieving individual not feel quite as "alone" during the process.

Resurrecting The Living

Prior to losing my own mother, I had a few close friends who lost theirs. During the time of their loss, I was there for them as moral support, offering prayers, positive thoughts, and a listening ear. However, until I lost my own mother, I didn't fully understand exactly what they meant when they proclaimed how losing a mother is one of the toughest losses a person can experience. These same friends would also proclaim how the loss of a mother presents an internal void a person will carry to their own grave. Of course, the effects are different for everyone, depending on the relationship they had with their mother or mother figure. Although I felt this may have been true, I didn't fully grasp those statements until my own mother actually passed away. I would empathize with them, but my empathy was limited. I felt sadness for them because they were my close friends, and no one who is a caring individual wants to see their friends hurting. I was always mindful that people grieve in their own timing and in their own ways. I was aware of this fact when I lost other family members early (i.e. my father, grandmother, and aunts and uncles with whom I had a close relationship).

Resurrecting The Living

Losing my mother was the most heart-wrenching loss I ever experienced. The mere fact that her loss left an unexplainable emptiness inside of me enabled me to understand what those same friends were trying to convey to me after their losses. Just as I had provided a listening ear to them, they all unselfishly returned the favor to me. They could truly empathize with this new void I developed suddenly. They were able to give me advice on various coping mechanisms, such as how they started celebrating Mothers' Day and their mothers' birthdays.

Since my mother's passing, I celebrate her birthday, Mothers' Day and the anniversary of her death each year in unique ways. On her birthday, I go out to dinner by myself and have a slice of coconut cake for dessert, which was her favorite cake. I also listen to one of her favorite songs, "Put Your Records On" by Corinne Bailey Rae. I always cook her favorite meal of homemade spaghetti on the anniversary of her death. I attempted to attend church the first two Mothers' Days after her passing. However, for the past three, I have resorted to staying home and reflecting on my relationship

Resurrecting The Living

with her, especially the life lessons she instilled in me.

Every person in their lifetime will experience loss. Whether it is the loss of a significant relationship (i.e. family member, friend, or pet), or circumstance (i.e. divorce, job loss, financial stability, or loss of identity), it is inevitable. How the person deals with, or refuses to deal with, the loss is an integral part of their emotional, psychological, spiritual and social growth. Sometimes, even disconnecting from society for a period of time can help the grieving individual re-evaluate, regroup, recharge and readjust their life. Of course, there are limits to disconnecting from others, such as going to work or the grocery store. Learning how to proceed without that person who has passed away is a daily challenge in the beginning.

I have had several disconnection periods since losing my mother. During those periods, I let certain friends and loved ones know, at least once a week, I am physically okay, so they won't worry about my well-being. During those times, I allow myself to feel whatever emotions hit me at a given moment. I take the time to let out the feelings in my own quiet time and personal space. These periods allowed me the space I needed to re-evaluate how and why I was feeling the way I was. It also enabled me to rearrange my thoughts and feelings in general, in terms of discovering ways of living each day without my mother and other recently departed loved ones; and to recharge and emerge into this brand new normal I had to begin facing for the rest of my life.

Once a person gets to a point where they are becoming somewhat adjusted to their new normal, they can help others experiencing grief and loss. My friends who lost their mothers prior to me losing mine were able to help me through the process. Now, as more of my friends and loved ones have lost mothers and others they were close to since my mother has passed, I can help them through their grief. I often reach out to old and new friends on social media whenever I hear of the passing of someone close to them. Not only do I reach out during that time, but I also try and reach out from time to time afterwards.

Helping others is an important characteristic my mother instilled in me. The pastor who performed the eulogy during her memorial service stated how my mother lived and touched many lives; and just as she touched many lives and lived out her true purpose on this Earth, now she has passed the torch along to me to continue to live my own life and do the same.

She loved and accepted people for who they were, and most of the time, that's all the average person needs. I am also passionate about and find joy in helping others in any way I can, whether it is through inspiration or helping them find resources for their basic needs. Using my personal story of grief is one of the main things I am very passionate about. I will continue to use my personal testimony in order to help others effectively cope with their own grief and loss.

Chapter 7

Resurrecting the Living
Acceptance and Finding a "New Normal"

Two very difficult, yet necessary stages in the grieving process are accepting the loss as a reality and finding a "new normal." By this, I am referring to rediscovering a new pattern of living life without those recently departed loved ones. This doesn't mean an individual has "gotten over" their loss; it means they have accepted the fact that the loved ones have passed away. They have also learned, of course in their own time, how to rearrange their usual routine of going about each day, week, month, year, and even moment devoid of the loved ones' physical presence.

Acceptance does not mean an individual has necessarily found happiness; but it does mean their depression has subsided tremendously. This stage is more of a stage of calm, where the person's emotions have eased up. The person may still have moments throughout their lifetime where they will fall into depression, feel guilt or anger, and will feel overwhelmed emotionally. This can be especially true each year during any special or significant occasion in which you may miss the presence of the deceased loved one.

To this day, I am still constantly reinventing my "new normal." My most recent relocation has been very pivotal in this process. Once I made this move, I ended up living just 10 minutes away from my god sister and her husband. She is not actually my "god sister"—she and I, along with her sister, have been very close friends—just like sisters—since we were all elementary and middle school-aged. Growing up, their house was the only house where I was allowed to stay overnight. Their parents have always been like second parents to me. I don't completely lean and depend on my god sisters and their family for everything, as I am very free-spirited and often maintain a pretty busy social calendar. However, they are a part of that social calendar many times and are always there for me whenever I need them, and vice versa. Additionally, I have a few close friends from my college days, as well as some friends I recently made at work and in my writers' group. These friends all live near me. I go to dinner, attend various events, and travel with my friends quite often. Being close to them makes for very strong social and familial connections.

I also visit other relatives quite often, such as my family in Spartanburg and my relatives on my father's side of my family. I keep in touch with my cousins on my mother's side periodically, as well as some of my stepfather's family, although most of us don't see each other as often as we did before our relatives' deaths. I have several families of close friends and relatives who have "adopted" me into their families as well. They all continue to play a major role in helping me through my grieving and healing process.

Family is very important to me. I have always depended on family for moral support in all of my

Resurrecting The Living

life's endeavors. Now that all of my parental figures have passed away, I continue to rely on my "circle" of friends and relatives for similar support. I don't expect any of them to "replace" my mother or other recently departed relatives; however, they have voluntarily maintained familial support for me. For example, I used to spend most holidays with my mother, aunt, uncle, stepfather and other relatives. I now spend holidays with either my god parents in Greenwood, my surviving relatives on both my mother's and father's sides, or a combination of all. I am thankful for their support, and I am now in an emotional and psychological space where I can reciprocate support to them whenever they need it.

As stated in a previous chapter, a grieving person needs to be surrounded by positivity. Once I reconnected to society after my disconnection periods, positive and inspirational social connections were paramount to my continued recharging and readjustment into my new normal. After all, the "social butterfly" couldn't remain in seclusion forever.

Traveling has become an integral part of my "new normal." When I visit various places, it gives me an exhilarating sense of exposure to a new environment and culture. It also enables a temporary "escape" from my grief and depression. My favorite types of "escapes" are areas near beaches. Being in the sand and by the water gives me a sense of calm and relaxation. It is a type of catharsis, and it helps me clear my mind and just "be." Living in South Carolina affords me the opportunity to take a day trip to a nearby beach whenever I deem it necessary.

In discovering a "new normal," it takes a lot of time and patience with yourself to figure out what works and doesn't work in your "new" daily life. Some people decide to continue a routine of some sort with their surviving friends and relatives, while others decide to temporarily disconnect from everyone to some extent. As in my case, some people may decide to relocate to a different area in order to get a fresh start of some sort. It may take several months or even years of trial and error to find your "new normal" and settle in it. You may also find yourself re-evaluating your new routine and either fine-tuning it or changing it completely throughout your lifetime. No one grieves the same, and the best course of action is to consult with your support system in finding whatever "new normal" will work for you.

Grief is, indeed, a part of life; yet, it is also a part of rediscovering and resurrecting the things inside of each individual that may have "died" with the departed loved one. I had to eventually be resurrected from the depth of my despair, pain and the dark place into a place of happiness, hopefulness and joy. The deaths of my mother, stepfather, aunt and uncle caused those things inside of me to die for a period of time. I didn't know that those things would ever come back to life, but they did over time and with lots of positive support.

My Mother

Jacqueline Johnson Quarles

January 23. 1941- August 27, 2013

About the Author

Roblynne McDuffie is an author and educator who resides in South Carolina. She earned her Bachelor's Degree in Sociology from the University of South Carolina-Columbia, as well as her Educational Specialist Degree in Counselor Education–K-12 School Counseling.

Roblynne is passionate about inspiring others through her personal struggles with depression, anxiety, grief, and loss.

Roblynne enjoys writing, traveling, dining out, dancing and live music.

www.ingramcontent.com/pod-product-compliance
Lightning Source LLC
Chambersburg PA
CBHW072057290426
44110CB00014B/1720